STOP School Violence. Say NO to Violence. STOP ABUSE

Nery Roman

ISBN-13:
978-1724512833

ISBN-10:
1724512838

Stop the Violence 2

Here's the big question after the horrible massacre in Las Vegas:

Why?

Sunday night, Stephen Paddock, from his room on the 32nd floor of the Mandalay Bay Casino, started shooting at the 22,000 people attending a country music concert. From his elevation, and with automatic weapons, it was like shooting fish in a barrel. A total of 59 died and more than 500 wounded. It is the worst mass shooting in recent American history.

Stephen Paddock, 64, is the son of Benjamin Hoskins Paddock who robbed two banks between 1959 and 1960. He was sentenced to 20 years in prison in 1961 — but escaped in 1968.

Benjamin Paddock, Las Vegas gunman's father, robbed banks and fled FBI, on NYTimes.com.

With his escape, Benjamin Paddock ended up on the FBI's most wanted list on March 18, 1969.

CAUTION

PADDOCK, DIAGNOSED AS PSYCHOPATHIC, HAS CARRIED FIREARMS IN COMMISSION OF BANK ROBBERIES. HE REPORTEDLY HAS SUICIDAL TENDENCIES AND SHOULD BE CONSIDERED ARMED AND VERY DANGEROUS.

The fact that Benjamin Paddock was diagnosed as psychopathic in 1969 is amazing. At that time, there was no standard way of diagnosing psychopaths. In fact, about the only book on the topic was Hervey Cleckley's Mask of Sanity.

Stephen Paddock was eight years old when his father was sent to prison. Benjamin Paddock was not in the lives of his sons as they were growing up.

Stephen Paddock attended college and worked for a predecessor company of Lockheed Martin. He eventually got into real estate and made a lot of money. In recent years, he was a professional gambler.

But he had no criminal record and was not violent. According to his brother, he had no political agenda and no religious affiliation.

Stephen Paddock, Las Vegas Suspect, was a gambler who drew little attention, on NYTimes.com.

The question remains: **Why did he do it? Was he a psychopath or a sociopath?**

From what's been released so far, only one psychopathic trait fits — it looks like Stephen Paddock had a need for excitement. He lived his life by gambling. He had a pilot's license and owned two airplanes. He also had hunting licenses.

After the shooting, we can say that Stephen Paddock must have had a lack of remorse, guilt or empathy — it's the only way he could kill so many people in cold blood. But were there indications of this before Sunday?

Stephen Paddock was a psychopath.

STOP The VIOLENCE

SAY NO TO VIOLENCE

STOP THE ABUSE

The book is dedicated to anyone who has gone through a traumatic event without the proper guidance and support to heal from the trauma.

I thank everyone who helped me create this book to create knowledge on psychopathy.

The book is written for anyone and it is easy to understand. It is a mix of personal information and book.

TRAUMATIC Event:

Introduction

Tile of the Book:

<u>Psychopathy: Terror in the Streets Other Side of Reality</u>

Trust "No One" when it comes to your children. SUSAN SAVAGE

A TRUE STORY LIVING WITH A PSYCHOPATH/SOCIOPATH AND CHILD MOLESTER

DO NOT KEEP QUIET WHEN YOU SEE AN ABUSE, IT DOESN'T MATTER WHO IT IS you need to TALK.

MY JOB IS TO CREATE AWARENESS.

There is not enough awareness of psychopathy/sociopaths and child molesters; this book will help millions understand who they are once we can identify them it creates a safer world for our children and our families.

I was condemned for telling

the truth.

No one will keep me quiet

now.

Reading this book should help uncover some of the mysteries of psychopathy/sociopath and child molester. Do not allow your children to talk to strangers on the internet.

The mother & the middle brother:

These two people are evil. Individuals who deal with them will eventually become their prey and will be irrevocable damage.

My mother's campaign is based on finding acceptance from other family members to accept the middle brother, the psycho, which makes her an "enabler" on whatever he does.

They fool me when I was a child, but they cannot fool me now. This is my time to tell my story and help others.

Never leave your child unattended, or with stranger's things tend to happen, and they do.

The book starts with an introduction.

You can become the new you, from victimization to the realization of whom we are dealing. It is important to know that these individuals can be very charismatic, loving, sweet, and like to help within the community, but most of all they want to get close to your child. You are no longer a victim; you are a survivor.

Be your own survivor, you can cure yourself, you can help yourself when no one else listens to you, you can become your new you.

They used me; they had no compassion and no empathy for their consecutive abuse and trauma; I have no compassion writing about them, and this information will help others…

I want to make clear: When I mentioned the word "family" in this book refers to the two brothers, mother, and passed father that's it. Other family members have nothing to do with the story, and they can't go after this writer since they are not part of this book, this book is only about my past and my past family the four people mentioned 2 brothers, 1 mother and 1 father.

Names used to create this book are fictitious to protect my real family, the story is true, and it was created to help create awareness to help other children, and families against psychopathy.

The more we are at peace with ourselves, the more we find peace with each other.

GOD HELPED ME AND MY FAMILY MOVE FORWARD WITH HEALTHY LOVE, AMEN...

Do NOT Allow your children to talk to EXTRANGERS in the internet without your supervision.

Sexual abuse has a long-lasting effect:

<u>*I grew up with Wolfs in the Wilderness*</u>

<u>*A Dark Beast to Tame.*</u>

<u>*Terror in the Streets*</u>

<u>*I know how they think? Do you? They are sick individuals.*</u>

Not everyone is bad, but we must learn about the sick, the psychopaths to become aware of the ones who are bad.

This story begins when this writer was eight years old. An innocent child raised in the wilderness by wolves. It took a couple of lessons in life to understand that I was raised by animals, in the middle of nowhere on a continuous attack by inside sources. My mother did not teach me anything about life; she never mentors me on what life was all about. She wanted to keep me as ignorant as possible in my early years, and that means danger for a child.

The book is a book that represents a battle for survival.

EXPRESS WHO YOU ARE IS NOT YOUR TIME

TALK

Freud used a concept as means to explain recurring patterns of self-defeating and self-destructive behaviors, which are called "repetition compulsions." Freud and Einstein "instinct and survival," letters suggested we must understand that there is no dark beast that we can tame, other that ourselves. The answers to the puzzles can be unraveled within us to survive. The mysteries of human beings and behaviors lie in how we as individuals and as societies counter balance our fears and aspirations. We all have the drive to compete, the need to care, a desire to connect and to be free. The answer lies in how individuals counter balance fears and aspirations, our drive to compete and our need to care. Einstein and Freud mentioned: "The more we are at peace with ourselves, the more we can create peace with each other.

Small Note of Awareness:

This story is a true overflowing with information dedicated to helping families with small children, based on provided examples and book. This book was written to create knowledge on psychopathy, important signs to look for in child molesters, childhood risk factors, female psychopathy, androcentrism, psychological consequences, the social skill child molesters and the conflict resolution on how to deal with psychopaths. To connect with the readers, this writer is using her personal experience to illustrate points related to psychopathy and child molesters. The middle brother, the psychopath and socially skilled child molester is on the loose; he is a danger to society. The mother believes him and protects him, which makes it worse for people who relate to the predator. This author has notified the authorities of Florida and due to The Statutes of Limitations a proper accusation against the aggressor was not approved based on age limitations and location where it occurred. It is this writer's responsibility to provide a testimonial to help others who might be in contact with the aggressor. He is also a socially skilled child molester and he sexually abused his little sister between the ages of 12 till 17. It is estimated that 50 percent of all sex offenses to children are not a result of pedophilia.

Awareness on Psychopathy:

This writer's main goal is to create awareness on psychopathy among men and women. This informational guide will make it simpler for men and women, especially families to identify the meaning of psychopathy and socially skilled child molesters. This book is a combination of book and samples of the author's personal life experience dealing with a psychopath.

It will also define the characteristics of psychopaths by providing examples to identify their world and what are the threats from those around us. How to prevent an attack from the silent snake; they know who they are, do we? The main purpose is to show readers how to recognize the different features psychopathy and how to differentiate them from others. It is important to find the unseen true face, behind their smile.

It will compare the experience of this author as a victim living with a psychopath and a social skilled child molester. This book is based on real evidence, an excellent source of information. It shows examples of psychopathy (personality disorder) and sexual manipulation. As a survivor living with a psychopath, examples will be provided in detail on his dysfunctional personality. The middle brother is just mentioned in this book several times, and his presence is only presented as a "sample," on what to look for on psychopaths and child molesters. "This writer's past is a new future for families." Unfortunately, when a child is left unattended or with someone considered "familiar," that we can trust, things do happen. "We cannot blind ourselves through the eyes of predators." Don't trust everyone when it comes to your children.

The resolution is to prevent this from happening again to another child. This writer has helped many people, especially women, at counseling. As parents protecting our children it's our main goal. Prevention is educating ourselves which means protection. We must educate ourselves for a brighter future, and for our children.

I would like to share my own values as human beings which are humility, family, truthfulness, integrity, unity, love, care, compassion and doing what is right. In the mind of a psychopath, not even half of these values exist. Ignorance is the worst nightmare when dealing with a true psychopath.

This book will help you recognize psychopath's characteristic, traits based on my personal experience. It wasn't an easy task to write this manuscript, but at the same time it is very informative. The book is divided into different sections. The chapters are based on explanations, literature review and characteristic of psychopaths. The important signs to follow, which are: oral communications, lying, childhood risk factors, manipulators, female psychopathy, a small explanation of androcentrism, the social skilled child molesters, psychological consequences, and the conflict resolution on how to deal with psychopaths and social skilled child molesters.

Table of Contents:

I.   Carl Jung quote and Psychopathy

II. *Violence in Schools ~ Psychopath Killers*

III. *Male Syndrome: Example of Androcentrism and Patriarchy*

IV. *What is Psychopathy?*

V. *Characteristics of Psychopathy: Theories*

VI. *Three important Signs to look for:*

      a. *Oral Communication*

      b. *Fibber*

      c. *Manipulators*

VII. *Childhood Risk Factors*

VIII. *Female Psychopathy*

IX. *Social Skilled Child Molesters*

X. *Psychological Consequences*

XI. *Hervey Cleckley's List of Psychopathy Symptoms*

XII.   *Conflict Resolution on how to deal with psychopaths.*

I. *Carl Jung & Psychopathy:*

Carl Jung in his book "Bad Men Do What Good Men Dream," everyone has a shadow which is part of the unconscious, and it contains repressed desires, weaknesses, and primitive animal instincts. Jung specified the less we acknowledge the "shadow," the less it is embodied in the individual's conscious life. The more we understand who we are, the more we can control those evil thoughts which makes less risk of being controlled by them.

This book is intended to identify the characteristics of psychopathy, signs to look for in psychopaths, the anatomy of the brain, child risk factors, female psychopathy, socially skilled child molesters, called "groomers" and the conflict resolution, violence against, women, men and children, and how to treat a psychopath. This book is primarily dedicated to families with small children. The author explains the practicality in today's world of patriarchy and androcentrism. This writer family was always dominated by father figure and two brothers, women and children were submissive. "Terror in the Streets Side of Reality," overflows with information and book to guide parents, and create consciously on what could happen to the "unattended child." Based on this writer's personal experience living with the middle brother who is a "child molester and psychopath." The middle brother results verified high probability on the PCL–R Psychopathy Checklist-Revised. His powers are to control and dominate. To manipulative, particularly the family and friends toward his advantage; exhibiting lack of emotion and remorse, glibness, superficial charm, pathological lying, poor behavior controls, promiscuous sexual behavior and many other factors establishes "the middle brother a full-blown psychopath. Hare (2003) checklist now called the PCL-R Psychopathy Checklist is meant to be used for trained mental health professionals who both interview and review the people's psychopathic history. Psychopathy is probably a factor for sure, in this case, a child was used as a "convenience" as a "toy" to satisfy the sexual urges of the perpetrator and his actions and character disorders make him a child molester and a psychopath.

Victims are the most powerful source of information to protect our children from child molesters. Individuals who have been sexually molested are the best "informants," because of our experiences. We can name the molester and can provide detailed information regarding the abuse. We tend to keep quiet for many different reasons, including fear, shame, and embarrassment. Telling about the abused was frightening, and it has continued to be frightening and emotionally difficult to express. This writer was never though the middle brother who is supposed to protect you will harm you in the nastiest ways. It is incomprehensible for this writer the actions of the middle brother towards a minor who was his sister. Too often, as victims, we failed to understand how their information can protect others; instead we continue to keep it a secret. On the other side, this *writer told her mother and oldest brother about the abuse and they disbelieve and did nothing towards the abuser; on the contrary, the mother keeps accepting the abuser. He is currently living in her home taking advantage of her low-income housing, and he keeps taking pictures with friends having a great time on Facebook. The writer's mother steady campaign to protect the abuser has made people think or believe something else. What reasons do this writer have to lie about these horrendous acts? What does this writer gain? Nothing! It is all true.*

Nevertheless, after telling my oldest brother about the abuse, he told me that was not true, and he has remained affectionate and in contact with the aggressor. The family has shown no sympathy towards the victimization. The middle older has full control and has been able to manipulate them. It is now up to this writer to help families and show his real mask; this book was built on personal experience dealing with a true psychopath. Terror in the Streets Side of Reality is a reference on how to deal with the other side, which hides, manipulates, exhibiting lack of emotion and remorse, glibness, superficial charm, pathological lying, poor behavior controls, promiscuous sexual behavior and many other factors established.

School VIOLENCE

Episodes of school violence are not new in the United States. The first school violence in American history happened in 1764 in the town of Greencastle, Pennsylvania (Dorn, 2013). Four men entered a school and shot the teacher and ten children. Subsequently, there have been numerous recorded instances of school violence. The riot school shootings at Columbine High School (1999), in which 13 people were killed, Virginia Tech University (2007), in which 32 people were killed, and Sandy Hook Elementary School (2012), in which 26 people were killed, stayed in the minds of the American people. Though the probabilities of a student being murdered in a school shooting are relatively small, (average 0.068 per 100,000 students) (Anderson,

2001) but it is a truth of the unexpected reality of a psychopath

killer. Prior to

these violence, people were not aware of this psychos and these acts

of violence until social media, tv newscast the information. A crisis

will be carried to millions of people through social media.

In the wake of numerous highly publicized school violence, students,

parents,

and educators have brought new levels of safety concerns forth.

Schools have instituted

numerous physical safety practices such as installing metal detectors

and hiring security

officers. Other safety procedures include video surveillance,

building access controls,

and badging, bulletproof glass, limiting entry and exit doors, and

signage

on the building stating there are police patrols (Fitzgerald, 2013).

Although enhanced

security measures have been implemented in many schools, safety

needs to be continually evaluated at every school as this threat

continues. The issue may never be

completely eliminated but every effort needs to be made to thwart a

possible school

shooting.

Numerous characteristics are known about deadly acts of violence

within schools.

These characteristics are:

- ✓ In ¾ of the incidents, one or more students/faculty were killed. More than ½ of the incidents occurred during the school day. 95% of the psychos were current students at the school.
- ✓ All the incidents were conducted by males. 81% of the incidents were carried out by a single attacker and a gun was used.

✓ *Events on school violence are rarely sudden, the student unexpectedly have a breakdown and commit these acts.*

✓ *Like more psychopath's killers, they obsessed on developing an idea and progressed towards achieving their goal.*

✓ *Most psychos engage in some behavior prior to the incident that caused others concern or indicated a need for help.*

✓ *Educators, parents, and schoolmates must be able to pick up on signals that are cause for concerns and feel that they can report what they see to someone that can help.*

✓ *There are many theories on how to attempt to identify those who might involve in targeted school violence. News reports of a school shooting have become almost a weekly headline.*

✓ *Violence is mostly pre-planned, and psychos often follow a pattern of "target*

  o *selection – surveillance - test to calculate safety - potential reexamination and*

  o *reconfirmation of the objective and desires - acquire access to attack.*

✓ *Incidents of targeted school violence are rarely sudden, impulsive acts (Vossekuil,*

✓ *2002). The student did not suddenly have a breakdown and commit these acts. They developed an idea and progressed towards accomplishing their goal. Most attackers engage in some behavior prior to the incident that caused others concern or indicated a need for help.*

✓ *Educators, parents, and schoolmates must be able to pick up on signals that are cause for concerns and feel that they can report what they see to someone that can help.*

There are many theories on how to attempt to identify those who might engage in

---

targeted school violence. The threat assessment process developed by the United States

Secret Service and the United States Department of Education (Fein, 2002) is a starting

point for schools to develop strategies to identify possible attackers prior to the attack.

One of the biggest fears for a parent when sending children off to school is the

possibility that a shooting will happen at that learning institution. According to Brock

(2009) one of the most critical issues facing the educational system in the United States

today is violence within schools. The school shootings at Columbine High School

(1999), Virginia Tech University (2007), and Sandy Hook Elementary School (2012)

show that shootings can happen at every level in the educational system.

With the threat of school shootings ever present, parents look to the school

administrators for guidance and assurances that their children are safe. Schools are

considered a safe place where children can learn, and teachers can educate without the

fear of gun violence (Dwyer, 2000). Parents need to be reassured that the educational

setting is secure. The school needs to be protected from threats from external and

internal sources. The protection from external threats can be accomplished through the

protective measures (Fitzgerald, 2013).

We need to protect the internal threat,

the school!!

I.   THE MALE SYNDROME: SMALL EXAMPLE ON ANDROCENTRISM

What is Androcentrism? Androcentrism is the practice of placing male human beings and the masculine point of view at the center of one's view of the world and its culture. The related adjective is androcentric, while the practice of placing the feminine point of view at the center is androcentrism. There is a correlation between psychopathy and androcentrism. When the male is seen as the ruler in a disturbed family, events tend to go wrong. My family was composed of two brothers, father, and mother who were dominated by the male syndrome, meaning "men" were the one who ruled, the ones who can treat anyone bad, especially women and we had to take it. No way! I replied. Androcentrism and Narcissist's personalities were always present in the family. After moving to Spain, I was no longer a little girl in the house, since the good family I left in Cuba was not there to protect me, now I was "estorbo." The family was highly motivated by "male," figure which made it easier for the psycho to attack and for them to believe he was the men of the house. How ridiculous, but true.

My mother did not have enough time to take care of me; she wanted to work, my father, on the other hand, was always drunk, so all he did was go out and drink with his buddies. I was in danger, but I was too small to recognize that I was in danger in my own home. Since they did not have anyone to take care of me, they used my middle brother (the psycho) do so during the day. Once I got out from school I will walk home from school, and he will be there waiting for me, like a pray. I was his prey, and he used me for his demon acts. Even though he had a girlfriend at that time, why not touch her, why used me as a toy, to practice? To practice by touching his little sister. He is sick and a bastard. I was 12 years old when he first attacked me, and he was 18 years old. A nightmare! He saw an opportunity from his sick mind and took it. Even though I know he is a bastard, clinically he is a psychopath/sociopath/child molester. Why kept his attention on me? Why so much fixation on me? Why can he just let me be and be the brother he needs to be like any other brother who cares and protects his little sister? The answer: he has a personality disorder, he is psychopath/sociopath/child molester who has a lot of issues and keeps hiding behind his mask. How sorry, I feel for the people who still believe this asshole. He will always be a bastard/asshole. I am a firm believer that people around you can help you cure or destroyed you completely. My husband has helped me get over some of my fears and grow emotionally. He has been part of my cleaning process, someone stable that cares about me.

This writer overheard someone stating, "he is such a nice, sweet person." A child molester sweet, lovable man? This is frightening, and sickening. It only proves how manipulative psychopaths can become, and they try to elicit compassion, the very quality psychopath's need. We can compare them to cats always marking their territory using their openness as a form of manipulation. Families manipulated by androcentrism domination, makes emphasizes on masculine interests or a masculine point of view only; centered or focused on men, often to neglect or exclusion of women and regard man or the male sex as central or primary. If we don't understand the psychology behind psychopathy, and their methods of operation, one cannot fully understand how to recognize a psychopath. This writer can recognize a psychopath by their glare, appearances, eyes, face, and conduct. Their diminutive eyes are part of their profile. It is sickening. Hiding behind his psychopathy, and some of them come across as a nice guy or a woman. They hide behind their own mask of insanity and their inability to see the other side of reality.

This writer's mother is unwilling to accept the fact, that he is a child molester and prefers to live an ignorant bliss with respect to the molestation incident. She facilitated for him the ability and the opportunity to molest his sister. They send me directly to the 'hands,' of evil. She is totally oblivious as to what happened, she refuses to recognize or acknowledge the situation. Her main job is to badmouth this writer's family by calling her crazy and a fabricator. Living in ignorance, believing it never happened, the abuse will go away. This writer is a firm believer that when the abuse was happening, she knew, but never confronted the situation and hides it. Her main motive was to hide the abuser and protect him from my father's aggressive behavior.

It is not a mental illness, and there is no mental incapacity; they can rationalize, and they have calculating minds, their minds are a game and their souls are evil. Psychopaths do learn from the past, but learn only what interests them interests, not what society wants them to learn (Samenow, 1984).

II. What is Psychopathy?

Psychopathy is a psychological condition in which the person

shows a profound lack of empathy for the feelings of others, a willingness

to engage in immoral and antisocial behavior for short-term gains, and extreme egocentricity. Psychopaths do not fear negative consequences of criminal or risky behavior and are relatively insensitive to punishment and people's feeling. They tend not to be deterred from their self-serving behaviors through criminal or social penalties. In conjunction with their unfeeling and incessant drive to take care of themselves, psychopaths are predators, and anyone who can feed their need is potential prey. A point of great concern is that these perpetrators are individuals responsible for the care and supervision of their victims. On November 20, 1989, the United Nations General Assembly adopted the Convention on the Rights of the Child, proclaiming elementary rights for children worldwide.

Psychopaths are at increased risk of engaging in both reactive and instrumental aggression. Instrumental aggression (sometimes called proactive or predatory aggression) is planned, controlled, and purposeful, and is used for an aim; for example, to get drugs or sex, or just to establish dominance. The primary goal is not necessarily to injure others but to obtain the desired outcome. The need to satisfy their needs is more important than anything else, including hurting others, some are also extremely aggressive. Aggression arises from an emotional reaction; it is the calculated use of aggression as a tool. Reactive aggression, on the other hand, is much more impulsive, and emotion-driven by a perceived

threat or attack or uncontrolled anger (Schouten & Silver, 2012).

Psychopaths are often superficially charming and glib; they are

frequently able to take advantage of others because they know that acting

genuinely friendly and helpful can be a useful strategy for getting what

they want (Schouten & Silver, 2012). To a psychopath, a punch in the face

and lie hidden behind a warm smile are merely separate tools to be

employed as dictated by circumstance. The bottom line is to not trust them.

Rather than being delusional or having difficulties perceiving reality,

psychopaths know exactly what they are doing. While it might be

preferable to assume that people who systematically commit unprincipled

acts somehow just aren't aware of the harm they are causing, the fact is

that psychopaths simply don't care whether they humiliate or injure others.

Nevertheless, some of them are not serious criminal, and sometimes they

know how to manage to avoid involvement with the criminal justice system.

Psychopaths sometimes are never apprehended by the police for the crimes

committed, various psychopaths know how to hide behind the law. What

saves them? The psychos can control his self-serving behavior, so they

remain perhaps just barely within the bounds of legal action, being *extremely manipulative with people helps and covering up their tracks, make it easier for them to escape. Also, being caught will "mean," they can't get away with what they want. Psychopaths and social skilled child molesters use their abilities to control and dominate their victims until the end. They tend to use friends, colleagues, and family members to cover their traits. It is frightening how they can be extremely manipulative, and controlling, understanding and learning how they are is the only way to survive.*

1) *Distinguishing Psychopaths and who they are?*

Characteristics of Psychopathy

- Theories

According to behavioral geneticist Dr. David Lykken (1995), psychopaths are apart from other deviants. This writer explored the history of childhood physical and sexual abuse, and the different personality categories of psychopathy. Brain studies suggested that psychopaths have abnormal brain activities. Psychopathy is defined as a constellation of affective, interpersonal, and behavioral symptoms that are characterized in an individual as being manipulative, charming, glib, irresponsible, selfish, callous, impulsive, aggressive, non-empathic, and experiencing little remorse or guilt because of one's injurious and antisocial behavior (Hare, 2003). Are neglected children more prompt to psychopathy? Children neglected are more at risk of psychopathy (Lykken, 1995). One should understand that psychopathy is not a mental illness but a personality disorder. Although, there is a subjective quality to diagnosing personality disorders, book has proven that those who have personality disorders display a rigidity or inflexibility in their thinking, feeling, and behaviors that impair them from functioning with others in a larger societal context (Cleckley, 1988).

Psychopathy is defined as a pervasive personality disorder, in which there is a disregard for the feeling of others and the rules of society (Cleckley, 1988). Personality disorders can be characterized by a class of personality types that deviate from societal expectations of acceptable behavior. Who are these people? Are gender comparisons well understood? We often think of psychopaths as the disturbed criminals whom capture headlines and crowd prisons (Hare, 1999). Psychopaths when caught, pass themselves as having psychological issues. Hare (1999) states psychopaths want others to believe that their antisocial ways are the result of mental deficiency; it was widely used as the "diagnostic bible" for mental illness.

Not all psychopaths are killers. Psychopath's men and women you might know that move through life with supreme self-confidence, but without a conscience.

Why is this worthy of the investigation? This book is based on this writer's personal experience as a molested child by a psychopath. This study will also help people who were victims of sexual abuse understand and identify psychopathic personalities and characteristics. Neumann (2007) discusses psychopathy as one of the most recognized personality disorder. This paper will present a well-balanced book comparative between women and men psychopathic behavior. Hare (2003) mentioned, that it is vital further book be conducted to identify which characteristics are most representatives of psychopathy between genders and how the syndrome is expressed. The conspicuous focus on psychopathic personality is in part due to its significant link with violence, aggression, and other externalizing pathology (Hare, 2003). This writer came across different theories that were developing to help explain the foundation of this personality disorder, and in doing so, several possible influences have been identified that facilitate the beginning facilitate of a psychopathic personality disorder. The purpose of this study is to examine and question the family environment factors, abuse history factors, and neurological factors have on predicting psychopathy.

Karpman's (1941) seminal article distinguishing between primary and secondary psychopathy provided the basis for subsequent theories and book on its variants. It is important to recognize Karpman (1941) theories of association between primary and secondary psychopathy. A primary psychopath wants everything; they are narcissistic, deviant and sneaky. Psychopaths are evil. Psychopaths can be cataloged as hunters stalking a prey, first, they find the right place to hunt, second, they realize the prey, third, catch the prey and lastly, use their pray for gruesome evil acts.

According to Karpman (1941), the principal distinction is based in etiology behavior. Karpman (1941) theorized that primary psychopaths are characterized by an affective deficit that is congenital, whereas secondary psychopaths are characterized by an affective disorder that develops because of dangerous interactions with the environment. Some psychopath displays signs of primary psychopathy involving personality traits such as egocentric, manipulative, deceitfulness, and lack of remorse toward his victims and the universe. Karpman (1941) said that secondary psychopaths exhibit their symptoms as an emotional adaptation to harmful factors in their home environments. Karpman (1941) argued that secondary psychopaths develop the traits of psychopathy to cope with such adverse conditions as abuse and parental rejection. Part of the reason for abuse is based on factors such as alcoholism, family abuse and neglect. Parents who exhibit an addiction to alcohol, or drugs are more likely to have children that develop psychopathy and other neurological disabilities.

Karpman (1941) also theorized that primary and secondary psychopaths differ in their core affective and interpersonal features and that their level of impulsivity and aggression may vary. Karpman (1941) argued that a secondary psychopathy carries with it underlying depression, anxiety, and character neurosis not present in primary psychopathy.

Dr. Hare (1999) describes psychopaths as predators who use charm, manipulation, intimidation and violence to control others and to satisfy their own selfish needs. Many use persuasions to get what they want, utilizing charm to intimidate and manipulate. This blameless *attitude, manipulation, and charm are used to show others they can be trusted, passing themselves as moral individuals. Psychopaths are skillful at saying one thing and doing another and telling people what they want to hear to buy time for their next scheme. They could be extremely influential toward others. Their inability to form attachments or empathize toward others (among other things) results in psychopathy.*

Karpman (1941) also believed that primary psychopaths have an "absent conscience," whereas secondary psychopaths have a "disturbed conscience." According to Karpman (1941), secondary psychopaths experience the same high level of hostility as primary psychopaths, but secondary psychopaths remain capable of experiencing higher human emotions such as empathy, guilt, love, or a desire for acceptance. Primary psychopaths are less impulsive than secondary psychopaths. Karpman (1941) also suggested that primary psychopaths often act instrumentally to maximize their own gain or excitement, whereas secondary psychopaths often act reactively from emotions such as hatred and revenge.

Karpman (1941) believed that this reactive response was a result of the secondary psychopath's underlying neurotic conflict. You might ask what is: "neurotic conflict?" As per Freud in general, a neurosis represents an instance where the ego's efforts to deal with its desires through repression, displacement, etc. fail. Also, it can be associated with the disorder, such as hypochondria or neurasthenia, arising from no apparent organic lesion or change and involving symptoms such as insecurity, anxiety, depression, and irrational fears, but without psychotic symptoms such as delusions or hallucinations.

Karpman's (1941) theory positioned this work for the further exploration of the originally hypothesized unitary constructs of psychopathy by 70% greater than the primary psychopaths 58%.

Three of the most important signs: They are abundant at oral communication, fibbers and manipulative.

1ˢᵗ) *Oral communication:*

Psychopaths know they are different, one important point they are excellent in oral communication and can jump into any conversation without shyness. As an example, one of the many signs of insanity once could be talking with friends; a psychopath will be able to get involved in a conversation without feeling of embarrassment. Some of them are motivated to read people, making friends and making sure they get what they want out of each friend or relative. It is very easy for them to gather enough information about you and find what you like or dislike. They can certainly know what your needs are, your drive, your attitude, your weaknesses, and vulnerabilities. They have an additional wisdom of life that we don't, since it is used for their own advancement. The world for them is a game, and all they do is move the toys around to win.

They can also switch keys until the find the right key to open the door; that will guide them where they want to be or what they need. Whatever the situation, they are always right, and we are wrong. They will act as if they are the victims and we are the bad guys that can't understand who or what their needs are. They are sharp in some ways but ignorant in others. They can't understand why we stopped talking to them, or calling them, why? I was such a nice friend, cousin, aunt, brother, sister? Why did they stop calling us? The answer is simple, we read this book, plus other books written by Hare and we got to know who you are.

After leaving my family for good, we moved to a different State. At this time, I won't disclose the information just for security purposes. In this new life, we found a couple of individuals that assured us were our new "friends." My husband liked them, and we enjoyed many visits to their house as well as them to ours. One day, in between those visits, we come across a big incident that marked our friendship forever. In this party, we bought some drinks, specifically Sangria and other eatable foods. At the end of the party, we gather together all our items to disembark. What was missing was the stuff we bought for the party, we thought. At arrival, my husband noticed that some of the items bought for the party were still in the car. The psychopath (sociopath) took the Sangria with him home to enjoy later in his home without letting anyone know. Other than being a psycho, he is extremely cheap. Why? Psychopaths play a game, and they always want to win. After buying all these items, they should have left them at the party for everyone to enjoy. This is an example of typical psychopath behavior disorder and the need to win and get something for them, at your own risk. For sure, after this incident they never saw us again. You never know what their next scam will be or pray...

2nd) Lying:

Why do they lie? It is hard to catch them on a lie, but nothing is impossible. Most people can't perceive their lies; they are based on a psychopathic lie. The lie serves many purposes to alleviate the distrusts or concerns of the victims and to strengthen their psychopathic fiction. As Hare mentioned in his book "Snakes in Suits," they are Artist at creating their convincing stories and explanations. These Artistic stories help them convince others by using entertainment and explanations or their face. These psychopathic individuals are immortal at not showing emotions, they can't feel; they have no face; they have no emotion and can project their stories with no facial expressions. Hare (2003) was precise when he says; they are "Artist" at creating their convincing stories and explanations. The main key to understand psychopath, look behind their mirror, and you should find. They are not only Artist, but also outstanding performers. More books should be written with another writer's experiences dealing with psychopaths.

How do we know who they are? Learning and reading more books and understanding the definitions of charming, artist, charismatic, out of the box and seeing them for what they are, psychopaths. In addition, we must remember they are psychopathic liars. Most observers do not see through the lies, but if we focus on the 'detail,' we should see their real identities.

Hare and Babiak mentioned lying and convincing others, and the use of charming explanations is done with the idea of reinforcing an environment of trust, acceptance, and a genuine delight. They become masters at lying and making others believe they are a sample to society. Their main purpose in life is to create acceptance and have others believe everything they say. This only gives them power to continue lying.

3rd) Manipulators:

Psychopaths are excellent at manipulating others. The middle brother used manipulation to build trust and had everyone in the family including my mother trusts all he said. He was the victim. They go after their prey, and little by little get what they believe it's theirs. With no feelings or emotions involved, they can continue to do what they want. It is a compulsion they won't stop until they get what they want. They like games. Their minds are set like a board game, manipulating their players. Manipulators are in their nature planned so that the offender can take advantage of others, even to reoffend against his original victim or other children. The manipulators most likely will use his personal set of circumstances to manipulate in unique ways. They are under surveillance it is harder for them to harm their victims, but without any person checking on them, their target comes easier. Sometimes these manipulators seek children, because they have never learned how to interact positively with adults. That's when the danger begins, and they must be stopped. Family members should be aware that offender manipulations often occur at transition points in the offender's life.

Manipulation by child molesters includes everything they do to try to control others without being open, honest, and direct about their true intentions. Psychopaths and child molesters particularly like to manipulate their victims, families, or anyone close to them whom they think they can get something out form them. They like to squeeze the juice of every situation or circumstance. In the case, we recently heard of Castro; he uses his manipulation to keep his victims in place, in control, and then he says in court he is not a monster, of course you were more a monster, you were

pure evil and a manipulator.

The ex-middle brother is such a manipulator, and he can outwit

the whole family with the help of my mother "the enabler," to think a good

person. He is not smart, not at all, but when it comes to evil and

manipulation they are devious. The best way to protect ourselves from

their evil manipulation is by talking, creating awareness, communicating

among everyone; this serves not only to keep our children safe, but the

community. Manipulation must be taken seriously; it can be catastrophic

for families. It is a toxic personality was the manipulator little by little

takes full control of his/her victims to later attack. I try hard to make the

family understand how dangerous the psycho could be, by providing

information about the offender and gathering information from what he

has done to others. If they are not able to believe there is not much I can

do, he has been able to manipulate them with the help of my mother's

campaign. At this time, I can only tell them what happened and whom they

are dealing with, but I cannot open their eyes or their minds for them, it is

up to us to see what is in front of us, to understand whom to trust, who not

to trust, and why. The results can be devastating for having the psychopath/sociopath/child molester in their lives. I can only do so much to help others, and thanks to the creation of this book I can help others.

4^(th)) Childhood risk factors

I remembered when we were small, how much he will bother me. He will hold my feet to stop me from walking around the house and I will cry a lot. I was always scared, very shy at the age of five. It will bother him that my mother's attention towards me was stronger than to him, since I was the little baby in the house. Middle children grow up with issues and feelings of abandonment. What I hear one day from one of my aunts was that he had a lot of trouble socializing with other. His issues started from an early age, and I am sure my mother knew based on his actions and hid them. I was too little to notice anything. The psychopathy does not miraculous appears later in life, children are born with this personality disorder. Book clearly indicate that the raw materials of the disorder can and do exist in children. The real problem is a persistent pattern of antisocial behavior during childhood and adolescence, such as violating social rules, aggression toward animals or other children, destruction of property, deceitfulness, theft, and serious rule violations. There are six different diagnoses used in the DSM-IV for childhood antisocial behaviors:

1.   Conduct disorders which involve a pattern of aggressive behavior toward people or animals, destruction of property, truancy, a pattern of deceitfulness, and/or serious violations of rules at home or at school.

2.   Oppositional Defiant Disorder (ODD) - Such children and adolescents usually exhibit a pattern of defiant and disobedient behavior, including resistance to authority figures, albeit not as severe as Conduct Disorder. This includes recurrent temper problems, frequent arguments with adults, and evidence of anger and resentment. Additionally, the defiant child/adolescent will often try to annoy others.

3.   Disruptive Behavior Disorder Not Otherwise Specific (DBD-NOS) - This is a category for those who show ongoing CD and ODD but who fail to meet the criteria for either diagnosis.

4.   Adjustment Disorder: With Mixed Disturbance of Emotions and Conduct - This is an array of antisocial behaviors and emotional symptoms that set in within three months of a stressor and fails to meet the criteria of the previously mentioned disorders.

5. Adjustment Disorder: With Disturbance of Conduct - This is like the other adjustment disorder, but with antisocial behaviors only.

6. Child or Adolescent Antisocial Behavior - This category is for isolated antisocial behaviors not indicative of a mental disorder.

Female Psychopath

Female psychopathy:

Female psychopathy is especially nebulous because, it is easily misinterpreted for normal dramatic female behaviors. Some social and behavioral sciences experts are willing to accept women may engage in reactive violence, such as engaging in self-defense; they refuse to accept the notion that females would be willing to take their time and plan a violent act.

The analogy reveals why it's so difficult for people to picture women as psychopathic predators (Pearson, 1998). All women are presumed to have a parental response, even if it's an anguished response or a crazy one. A woman who grows wild and furious with her child, her act is interpreted as an engagement (Pearson, 1998). What if the child has no ability to affect her at all? That child is invisible, annihilated. The most dreadful cases of child abuse are the ones in which a child was ignored or neglected. Nothing can be so threatening to one's remembered childhood ego as the idea of maternal indifference and neglect, not just by psychopaths; this is one of the most common forms of maternal aggression (Pearson, 1998).

Although men are more likely to show characteristics of psychopathy than women, Cleckley (1988) included female subjects among the prototype cases in the Mask of Sanity, suggesting that the full syndrome of psychopathy occurs in both genders. According to psychopathy expert

Hare (1999), there are many clinical accounts of female psychopaths, but relatively little empirical book. This writer believes gender stereotypes and sex role judgments are some of the causes for lack of book on female psychopathy. Some individuals tend to connect antisocial behaviors of women as a form of personality disorder or borderline disorder.

When compared to data provided by Hare (2003) for male offenders, differences in the factor loadings of individual items from the PCL-R have been found in female offender samples. Hare (2003) explains that similar studies using self-report-based measures comparison of psychopath suggest that male tend to score higher on these measures that female although this pattern is qualified by the handful of studies finding no significant gender differences. It is very interesting how Hare (2003) goes on and demonstrates the generality of psychopathy and its measures across gender; it is also necessary to consider the comparability of instrument structure and item functioning.

As explained by Hare (1999), the inconsistency in factor structure across gender could reflect limitations of the original two factor model. Hare (2003) and his colleagues conducted a detailed examination, using a four-facet model with 138 female inmates. The results found counter to suggestions that psychopathic individuals may not benefit from treatment and its raises the possibility of gender differences in treatment response (Hare, 2003). Women psychopaths are ranked as narcissistic. They use others as means for their own gratification and dump them when no longer needed. Women psychopaths always take, never give. Female psychopaths use sympathy as prey on others. They are the victim. They prey on weakness they see in others. They look weak, pitiful to garner attention and compassion to lower the guard of the intended victim. Also, some females use sex as a hook to juggle multiple victims into tangled relationships. As an example, in the movie Heart Breakers release, in 2001, both women drained their victim's energy and money until they served no purpose.

Also, Hare (2003) explained, inconsistent findings across gender regarding the relation between psychopathy and criminal and violent behavior. This finding may reflect broader inconsistencies in the development of antisocial and aggressive behavior across gender. He recognizes that gender differences in the development of aggression across childhood and adolescence may contribute to differences in base rates of psychopathy across gender; He also found less powerful prediction of violence in female than in male samples. Hare (2003) states, only a few studies, have been conducted to examine the relationship between psychopathy per se, as opposed to criminality and incarceration and other forms of psychopathology in women. Another recent example is Jody Arias is a cold-blooded murder and a psychopath. She is very calculated and a manipulator. Her main goal is to win and not getting caught. Arias in the beginning got closed to the investigators to find out what was going on, lying to them. Psychopaths get a thrill on getting very close to their victims or thinking they are getting away with murder. Jody Arias was getting a thrill by getting close to investigators, without getting caught. Her main goal was "not" to get caught; that's her goal. She can easily disconnect from reality. Aria's awkward behavior, immaturity, egocentric and narcissistic personality are all part of her psychopathy. She is a dishonest individual, psychopath trying to get away with murder. When she wants to get out of something, then she cries or gets a headache. Arias cries, not for what she did, probably she cries because she is feeling sorry for herself. "It is all about her." Sometimes is hard to see Jody Arias as a psychopathic killer, they said: "she is beautiful." Looks have nothing to do with women and men psychopathy; it's all related to their brain function. Arias' suffers from borderline personality disorder and psychopathy.

Sometimes people who suffer from borderline personality disorders don't cover up their tracks; they kill themselves after they have committed such evil acts. What is a borderline personality disorder? The main feature of borderline personality disorder (BPD) is a pervasive pattern of instability in interpersonal relationships, self-image and emotions. People with borderline personality disorder are also usually very impulsive.

This disorder occurs in most by early adulthood. The unstable pattern of interacting with others has persisted for years. Relationships and the person's emotion may often be characterized as being shallow.

A person with this disorder will also often exhibit impulsive behaviors and have most of the following symptoms:

❖ *Frantic efforts to avoid real or imagined abandonment*

- *A pattern of unstable and intense interpersonal relationships characterized by alternating between extremes of idealization and devaluation*

- *Identity disturbance, such as a significant and persistent unstable self-image or sense of self*

- *Impulsivity in at least two areas that are potentially self-damaging (e.g., spending, sex, substance abuse, reckless driving, binge eating)*

- *Recurrent suicidal behavior, gestures, or threats, or self-mutilating behavior*

- *Emotional instability due to significant reactivity of mood (e.g., intense episodic dysphoria, irritability, or anxiety usually lasting a few hours and only rarely more than a few days)*

- *Chronic feelings of emptiness*

- *Inappropriate, intense anger or difficulty controlling anger (e.g., frequent displays of temper, constant anger, recurrent physical fights)*

- *Transient, stress-related paranoid thoughts or severe dissociative symptoms*

- *As with all personality disorders, the person must be at least 18 years old before they be diagnosed with it.*

- *Borderline personality disorder is more prevalent in females. It is thought that borderline personality disorder affects approximately 2 percent of the general population.*

- *Jody Arias past living with her parents was abusive towards her, because they wanted to control her life, and she wanted to do whatever she wanted. She mentions she was physically abused by her parents when she didn't do what they expected of her, which made their relationship abusive.*

Social Skill Child Molesters:

"A psychopath invents reality to conform to his needs" (Grondahl, 2006). This writer book on psychopathy personality categories did not

considerably differ on a history of physical or sexual childhood abuse, yet a greater proportion of secondary psychopaths endorse a history of physical and sexual. Cleckley (1988) mentions that whether judged in the light of his conduct, of his attitude, or of material elicited in the psychiatric examination, shows no sense of shame. This writer older male sibling showed no sense of emotion or care of the abuse as well as no signs of remorse; he was motionless as nothing ever happened. Cleckley (1988) explains psychopaths are always full of exploits, any one of which would wither even the more callous representatives of the ordinary man. He does not, despite his able protestations, show the slightest evidence of major humiliation or regret (Neumann, 2007).

This writer older (middle child) male sibling lacks the moral standards and humanity. His behavior was always one of superiority. His reality was built to his advantage, with no remorse or consequences behind his actions. This writer can fully appreciate and understands his cruel psychopathy, thanks to this book psychopathy, a personality disorder; part of his actions and behavior; an opportunistic and a psychopath that was free to do what he wanted who got away. He is a classic psychopath. Hare (1999) mentions psychopath's lack in conscience and feelings for others;

they cold-blooded take what they want and do as they please, violating social norms and expectations without the slightest sense of guilt or regret.

The recent book about psychopathy indicates that there is a relationship between psychopathic personality disorder and some form of sexual violence adolescence (Shohov, 2002). Shohov (2002) also notes, the relationship between child molesting and psychopathy is much less clear. Based on the book finding, we argue that some sex offenders can be classified as sexual psychopaths, criminals whose sexually deviant behavior is directed at diverse victim profiles and who are primarily motivated by thrill- seeking and opportunity (Shohov, 2002). This book contributes to a better understanding of such individuals will inform and improve this process. A factor focus significantly in crime and sexually deviant behaviors, which are the constellation of characteristics known as psychopathy (Shohov, 2002). For sexual psychopaths, we argue that it is a sexual element and the victim type that are or at that point in time the object of the violent thrill-seeking (Porter 2000).

Porter (2000) hypothesized that psychopathic individuals are over-represented in offenders who offend sexually against a variety of victim types. The most basic classification system of sex offenders distinguishes child molesters and rapists (Shohov, 2002). Child molesters are opportunistic, in conditions and settings to commit their crimes. Molesters seek out easy targets, mostly children, whom they know, and they have established a relationship. This author's middle male sibling spotted an opportunity to satisfy his sexual urges and took it. I was left abandoned with no parental supervision, his psychopathy predispositions were made easier for him to please. On the other hand, for the psychopath, the primary subsistence is to lie, with no physiological reactions. Lying is their primary weapon. The lie is the justification in their heads that they have the right to cause harm and lying are as natural as breathing for them. Psychos when caught in a lie, try to escape by creating more lies.

Who are the "Groomers?" They are the first ones who ingratiate themselves with adults for the express purpose of being given free access to children by innocent but ignorant adults (Van Dam, 2006). Child molesters also gravitate to those who are most likely to be too polite to fend them off, too shy and anxious to tell them to leave, too dependent to be assertive, and too impressed by rank, power, status, or money to do the right thing (Van Dam, 2006). Child molesters deliberately associate with adults who cannot address these issues. They seek out adults who worry about hurting people's feelings. They charm adults who do not believe it could happen. Dam (2006) mentions in her book "The Socially Skilled Child Molesters," the children most at risk of being sexually abused by these Groomers are the children surrounded by adults who cannot stomach learning about child sexual abuse (Van Dam, 2006). These adults may, therefore, inadvertently be more likely to welcome child molesters into their homes, organizations, or communities, ignore the evidence, overcome concerns, and talk them out of believing possible suspicions (Van Dam, 2006). Child molesters who are addicted to having sex with children are, therefore, more likely to appear wherever children congregate. Sometimes all they need to do were get on chat and set an appointment with a child with no parental permission. The unattended child is more prompt of the abuse than the children who are constantly under parent's shields. Some groomers take grooming one step farther and groom people outside the home. Grooming the social environment remains even after an offender admits or is sentenced. The offender, in this case, the middle brother offered to take care of his little sister to get the change to abuse her. He used denial to escape from the situation. It is a characteristic most of the sex offenders and child molesters denied what they did.

This writer is providing an example of the middle sick brother and grooming. This is a piece of the story that relates to grooming. It is important to understand that psychopaths are extremely manipulative. They suffer from a personality disorder and child molesters groom their victims.

The psycho and child molester abused me several times at small and older age. It occurred when we moved from Cuba to Madrid, Spain. The middle brother was never a brother who will give a damn about his little sister. He will never take me out for a walk or talk to me. Until the day, he started grooming and abusing this victim. When I was a child no one paid much attention to this writer, except for some cousins in Madrid. My mother and father were not the typical conversational type and did not pay much attention to me. The older brother was always doing his own thing and never paid attention to me. For the older brother to take me out was a fiasco, he disliked taking care of me. So, the psycho knew he will succeed at grooming this writer. It will be an easy task for him to do. I was left in the hands of Evil.

At the age of ten, twelve and thirteen my development changed very quickly, and the middle brother realized it. It is very sick, but that's how they think, only about themselves. He never spoke to me until that day.

I was surprised that he never spoke to me before and started talking about

Superman. As a child, I used to love Superman, and I had a poster of him

in my room. One day he walked inside my room and talked to me about

Superman and said nice things about him, and that he will buy one more

poster of Superman just for me. Grooming process took him a week or two

and then he started to take my clothes off. At the age of twelve, this writer

had no idea what he wanted. He gradually took off my clothes and abused

me at the age of twelve, thirteen, fourteen, fifteen and seventeen. The child

molester is almost six years older than this writer; at that time this

happened, he was probably twenty-two and twenty five. He was a grown up

sick man. He knew what he was doing. He used to show me pornographic

magazines at the age of eleven and will ask me to open my leg and pose

like the girls in the magazines. He is not only a child molester, but also a

groomer, psychopath, and a bastard. You don't do that to your little sister

or anyone, children are not born to be abused not by their brother or

anyone. The grooming stopped at the age of fourteen. I think one day he

got tired of his grooming game, and one day tries to touch me in front of

my mother and older brother. The older brother said to him "little sisters are not to be touched." My mother saw him and realized what was going on and placed me in a Daycare's thinking this will stop his sick behavior toward me. My mother never said anything to my father, since she knew he would have killed him. This was the worst alternative and action she could take since he continued with the abuse. He is a pig and the devil. I could survive living among wild animals because I'm better than them.

As an abused child, we are less experienced in decoding facial expressions. Book suggests abused children are less skilled in decoding facial expressions. The resolution for this abuse is treatment, but even with therapy does the abuse ever stop? It never stops, treatment doesn't work. What works is the prison, identifying their characteristics of psychopathy/child molesters and get away from them helps.

DECLINE in SEXUAL LIBIDO:

The offender may experience a decline in his sexual libido, but this is only from being caught and is only temporary. This decline in sexual libido is called "the monastic effect," which is based on the myth that monks do not have a significant sexual libido and therefore do not engage in sexual activity. This effect is short-lived, psychologists who do not deal directly with the sexual issues may take the monastic result as a cure. This is a mistake that should not happen. The child molester can use the monastic effect and his/her psychopathy to make others believe they are cured when they are not. These people need therapy for their entire life and existence; child molesters do not get cured in one day.

Psychological consequences

This writer has reinforced powerful influence "toughness." Sexually abused women suffer physically, psychologically and emotionally. This writer refuses to be a victim. This writer was an abused child at the age of twelve and suffered from attention deficit disorders and post-

traumatic stress disorders. Survivors of sexual abuse may also experience "dissociation" an impressive defense mechanism formed during ongoing sexual abuse, in which the person being abused "leaves", his body, and watched the abuse from some higher viewpoint. Victims tend to be their own worst enemies since they can damage themselves by the things they do.

Survivor connection with others: The AFTER EFFECT:

Because the survivor is focusing on issues with identity and intimacy, she often feels like a second adolescence. The survivor who has grown up in an abusive environment lacks the social skills that usually develop during this stage in life. The awkwardness ad self-consciousness and self-consciousness that make normal adolescence tumultuous and painful are often magnified in adult survivors, who may be ashamed. Adolescent style of coping may also be prominent at this time.

The Disrupted Relationship:

In a climate of profoundly disrupted relationship, the child faces a formidable developmental task. I had to find a way to form myself again that is part of the resolution. I must find a way to develop a sense of basic trust and safety with everything around me. I must develop my own sense of self in relation to others who are helpless, uncaring, or cruel towards me. I had to develop my own body self-regulation in an environment in which my body was at the disposal of somebody else in the family, my middle brother, the psycho. As a small child, I did not know what was going on and what they were doing to me; I had to develop an environment of initiative where I bring a will of complete conformity with the abuse and the abuser. On the other hand, the abuser must do the same; his job of hiding is formidable, that only a psychopath could do. I find myself abandoned without mercy; I must find trust in myself, to preserve hope and meaning. I survived, like many captive individuals who are abused must go along with the abuse, neglect, and terror. I didn't know better, at the age of eleven I couldn't just run and get out, I had to say home and keep believing that there was nothing wrong with my parent's neglect, there was nothing wrong with the sexual abuse. I said, "This is a secret I need to keep from both of us, this was the only form of love I got at that time and the only attention." That this was part of growing up, this was love giving in a different way, or form. After living my own native country to go to a new country, being neglected by my parents, I was left in the hands of evil, my only escape was to take the pain, take the abuse, and endure the agony.

When you have been sexually abused sometimes you feel guilty and shameful; the reason is age, I couldn't judge between right and wrong. In some "cultures," people think the child should react, and say no, but sometimes the grooming process goes beyond stopping the abuse. It happened when I was twelve years old, when a child is undeveloping. This writer couldn't comprehend what the psycho middle brother was doing with my body and why? This writer was very young, neglected, shy and unprotected by her parents. I suffer from low self-esteem.

I was able to survive by not giving up hope. Therefore, I founded people that listened and understand my story. Found compassion from friends and strangers, then my own flesh and blood. I exercised compassion toward others and learned how to live a life free from pain.

Related to dissociation is sexual "numbness," which is the outcome of a child willing her body to numb itself against arousal during unwanted touch (Scott, 2008). Unfortunately, this defense mechanism may result in a feeling of dissociation during desired sexual activity with a loved one later in life.

When women have been molested as children, the aftereffects can be far-reaching. Current relationships may be adversely affected. The giving and receiving of emotional or physical intimacy are often compromised. A woman's fears may project her feeling to her children.

Additionally, other disorders as the result of severe abuse in childhood are depersonalization disorder. This can be of a physical, emotional, or sexual nature.

Findings in 2002 indicate that an emotional abuse is a strong predictor of depersonalization disorder in adult life, as well as of depersonalization as a symptom in other mental disorders; analysis of one study of 49 patients diagnosed with depersonalization disorder indicated higher scores than the control subjects for the total amount of emotional abuse endured and for the maximum severity of this abuse (Scott, 2008). The bookers concluded that the emotional abuse has been relatively neglected by psychiatrists compared to other forms of childhood trauma (Scott, 2008).

Conclusion: Conflict Resolution:

This writer is working on a conflict resolution to let go of all the irritation, anger, resentment, upset, and disappointment. There is not much we can do about our past, but we can change our children future by caring for them. It helped me write this book and gather all the theories and information. It helped me as a victim see the other side of reality, the reality of the abuser, the psychopath. For practical reasons, most people rely on how people should act. The experiences of dealing with a child *molester and psychopath help me understand his deceitful tracts. He knows how to hide behind his mask, and his manipulation makes him an expert on gaining the acceptance of others. It does not matter how many times I explain my story, readers will understand the story once they are exposed face to face with the predator; and even when we confronted the predators, we might not be able to see through them. Their psychopathy is hard to find and catch. The offender has always hidden the truth about himself from others. He has also deliberately revealed parts of his life that would decrease suspicion. He has learned how to read others' reactions and change his way to gain acceptance. He is a skillful deceiver. People who deal with him daily must learn the basic steps to recognize his deliberate deception. The resolution for this write was to write this book and create awareness based on her personal experience living with a psychopath. At the same time, thanks to this book, I was able to learn more in-depth what are the characteristics of a psychopath. This book was an eye opener for this writer and many readers. The relationship with them should be based on skepticism. Lykken (1995) contends that most antisocial behaviors in children are caused by poor parenting absent fathers and inadequate mothers who neglect their children. Perhaps the child frustrates them or perhaps their parenting skills are subnormal and either way, the child acts out (Lykken, 1995). Lykken (1995) calls these children sociopathic, and he considers that we can decrease their numbers with better social skills at home. It is up to parents to do this, and where parenting fails, the child with those traits may express them through violence (Lykken, 1995). This author's opinion, child prone to psychopathy can be guided through good parenting by using traits in pro-social ways. They live in all cultures. Karpman (1948) believed that, as a result, only secondary psychopaths are amenable to treatment because their behavior is acquired and based on an underlying conflict and that, therefore, they possess the capacity to live moral and ethical lives. Clearly, these types of cheating strategies (which also consist of lying, swindling, cunning, deception, etc.) are commonly used by psychopaths in their everyday lives, and normally work well for them, particularly in gaining access to mates and resources necessary for survival (Hare, 1993). Parents, in appropriate, sensitive ways, teach your children of the potential danger of abuse and how to avoid it. Be aware of warning signs, such as an abrupt change in a child's behavior, which may signal a problem and be alert to a child's unsettled feelings and identify their origin (Scott, 2008).*

This writer's personal journey in booking and analyzing psychopathy has led to a cathartic and eye-opening revelation. Had this disorder been recognized or diagnosed before this writer's unfortunate experiences as an innocent child, it would have saved this writer from mental anguish and psychological fallout. Conflict resolution for this situation can only happen when family members such as a mother, brothers and close relatives understand and recognize the pathology of personality disorder such as psychopathy. To stop and avoid a recurrence of the incidences which occurred to this writer, an intervention of sorts must be conducted to expose the middle male disorder.

Should this conflict resolution occur, the ability to the see "the other side of reality" is what will save us from the violence of a psychopath. We need to see them for what they are and not for what they try to represent. The present is important; the past is gone; working on the traumas from the past makes us a better person for society today. Once we come to the realization of what have happened to us, we cannot harm ourselves anymore. It is time to recover and become the new you.

Resolution after the Trauma:

After the trauma diminishes into the past, it no longer represents a barrier to intimacy. At this point, I am no longer a victim but has become a new survivor. Relationships in the future are ready to establish with energy and new ideas. If the victim has been involved in a relationship during the recovery process, it becomes easier to go through the process with a partner. The partner helped me with the trauma.

The resolution of the trauma is never final, and recovery is never complete. The impact of the traumatic event will continue through the survivor's lifecycle. It is up to the survivor to find help to recover, but most important to find peace and understanding on what have happened. Conflicts that were sufficiently resolved at one stage of recovery will stop reoccurring and will disappear. The reason for the creation of this book was to help the victims find resolution. The truth many of us have traumatic memories, but there is a point in our lives that we can say: "Today I will stop the suffering; today I will not grieve anymore."

"Today is my time to be happy." Forgive yourself and create a new life for you today. We cannot allow memories to hunt us or allow them to make us feel miserable. We are the rulers of our lives, and we have the power to change who we are. Today is the day to feel good about yourself, to be you and accept other for what they are and how they are. We need to repeat to ourselves that we are good, we are no longer the victims; we are the survivors, and we are here on this earth to endure our traumas, learn from them, and move on. I understand sometimes it is not easy to move on, but it must be done to survive and have a better life than the life of the abuser. Even though the resolution is never complete, it is often sufficient for me as a survivor to turn my attention to the task of ordinary life.

As per book Trauma and Recovery by---------- the following stages should be followed, and they are all interconnected. There is no order on how we manage these stages; the survivor goes through some of these stages. One can come before the other; there is no order on how to manage our feelings and victimization. The most important part of the process is to be thankful for your current life and for the changes you have completed and graceful for what you have now, that is part of the recovery system.

1) *Psychological symptoms of post-traumatic stress disorder have been manageable or non-existence*

2) *Able to control feelings associated with the traumatic stress or abuse, etc...*

3) *The person has the authority to manage her/his memories, and decide when to bring them out and when to hide them on the side*

4) *Narrative memories linked with feelings*

5) *Self-esteem has been restored = this must be worked daily, is one of the hardest to restore.*

6) *Important relationship has been established or reestablished.*

7) *The person has reconstructed a coherent system of meaning and belief that encompasses the story of the trauma.*

8) *My theory: change your minds, change your thinking will help change who you are by being positive and do not be afraid to be yourself.*

DECLINE in SEXUAL LIBIDO:

The offender may experience a decline in his sexual libido, but this is only from being caught and is only temporary. This decline in sexual libido is called "the monastic effect," which is based on the myth that monks do not have significant sexual libido and therefore do not engage in sexual activity. This effect is short lived, psychologists who do not deal directly with the sexual issues, may take the monastic result as a cure. This is a mistake that should not happen. The child molester can use the monastic effect and his/her psychopathy to make others believe he is cured, when they are not. These people need therapy for their entire life and existence; child molesters do not get cured in one day.

Psychological consequences

This writer has reinforced powerful influence "toughness." Sexually abused women suffer physically, psychologically and emotionally. This writer refuses to be a victim. This writer was an abused child at the age of twelve and suffered from attention deficit disorders and post-traumatic stress disorders. Survivors of sexual abuse may also experience "dissociation" an impressive defense mechanism formed during ongoing sexual abuse, in which the person being abused "leaves", his body, and watched the abuse from some higher viewpoint. Victims tend to be their own worst enemies since they can damage themselves by the things they do.

Survivor connection with others: The AFTER EFFECT:

Because the survivor is focusing on issues with identity and intimacy, she often feels as a second adolescence. The survivor who has grown up in an abusive environment lacks the social skills that usually develop during this state in life. The awkwardness ad self-consciousness and self-consciousness that make normal adolescence tumultuous and painful are often magnified in adult survivors, who may be ashamed. Adolescent style of coping may also be prominent at this time.

The Disrupted Relationship:

In a climate of profoundly disrupted relationship, the child faces a formidable developmental task. I had to find a way to form myself again that is part of the resolution. I must find a way to develop a sense of basic trust and safety with everything around me. I must develop my own sense of self in relation to others who are helpless, uncaring, or cruel towards me. I had to develop my own body self-regulation in an environment in which my body was at the disposal of somebody else in the family, my middle brother, the psycho. As a small child, I did not know what was going on and what they were doing to me; I had to develop an environment of initiative where I bring a will of complete conformity with the abuse and the abuser. On the other hand, the abuser must do the same; his job of hiding is formidable, that only a psychopath could do. I find myself abandoned without mercy; I must find trust in myself, to preserve hope and meaning. I survived, like many captive individuals who are abused must go along with the abuse, neglect and terror. I didn't know better, at the age of eleven I couldn't just run and get out, I had to say home and keep believing that there was nothing wrong with my parent's neglect, there was nothing wrong with the sexual abuse. I said, "This is a secret I need to keep from both of us, this was the only form of love I got at that time and the only attention." That this was part of growing up, this was love giving in a different way, or form. After living my own native country to go to a new country, being neglected by my parents, I was left in the hands of evil, my only escape was to take the pain, take the abuse, and endure the agony.

When you have been abused you feel guilt and shameful; the reason is age, I couldn't judge between right and wrong. It happened when

I was twelve years old; the child is undeveloped to control. This writer couldn't comprehend what the psycho middle brother was doing with my body and why? This writer was very young, neglected, shy and unprotected by her parents. I suffer from low self-esteem.

I was able to survive by not giving up hope. Therefore, I founded people that listened and understand my story. Found compassion from friends and strangers, then my own flesh and blood. I exercised compassion toward others and learned how to live a life free from pain.

Related to dissociation is sexual "numbness," which is the outcome of a child willing her body to numb itself against arousal during unwanted touch (Scott, 2008)? Unfortunately, this defense mechanism may result in a feeling of dissociation during desired sexual activity with a loved one later in life.

When women have been molested as children, the aftereffects can be far-reaching. Current relationships may be adversely affected. The giving and receiving of emotional or physical intimacy is often compromised. A woman's fears may project her feeling to her children.

Additionally, other disorders as the result of severe abuse in childhood are depersonalization disorder. This can be of a physical, emotional, or sexual nature.

Findings in 2002 indicate that an emotional abuse is a strong predictor of depersonalization disorder in adult life, as well as of depersonalization as a symptom in other mental disorders; analysis of one study of 49 patients diagnosed with depersonalization disorder indicated higher scores than the control subjects for the total amount of emotional abuse endured and for the maximum severity of this abuse (Scott, 2008). The bookers concluded that the emotional abuse has been relatively neglected by psychiatrists compared to other forms of childhood trauma (Scott, 2008).

Conclusion: Conflict Resolution:

This writer is working conflict resolution is to let go of all the irritation, anger, resentment, upset, and disappointment. There is not much we can do about our past, but we can change our children future by caring for them. It helped me write this book and gather all the booked information. It helped me as a victim sees the other side of reality, the reality of the abuser and psychopath. For practical reasons, most people rely on how people should act. The experiences of dealing with a child molester and psychopath help me clearly understand his deceitful tracts. He knows how to hide behind his mask, and his manipulation makes him an expert on gaining the acceptance of others. It does not matter how many times I explain my story, only others will understand it when they are face to face with the predator and even when we are confronted with the predators we might not be able to see through them. Do to their psychopathy they are hard to catch. The offender has always hidden the truth about himself from others. He has also deliberately revealed parts of his life that would reduce suspicion. He has learned how to read others' reactions and gauge when others might be suspicious. He is a skillful deceiver. People who deal with him daily must learn the basic steps to realize his deliberate deception. The resolution for this writer was to write this book to create awareness based on her personal experience living with a psychopath. At the same time, this writer was able to learn based on the book what are the characteristics of a psychopath. This book was an eye opener for this writer and many readers. As like alcoholic's sex offenders never cure. The relationship with them should be based on skepticism. Lykken (1995) contends that most antisocial behaviors in children are caused by poor parenting absent fathers and inadequate mothers who neglect their children. Perhaps the child frustrates them or maybe their parenting skills are subnormal and either way, the child acts out (Lykken, 1995). Lykken (1995) calls these children sociopathic, and he considers that we can reduce their numbers with better social skills at home. It is up to parents to do this, and where parenting fails, the child with those traits may express them through violence (Lykken, 1995). This author's opinion, a child prone to psychopathy can be guided through good parenting by using traits in pro-social ways. They live in all cultures. Karpman (1948) believed that, as a result, only secondary psychopaths are amenable to treatment because their behavior is acquired and based on an underlying conflict and that, therefore, they possess the capacity to live moral and ethical lives. Clearly, these types of cheating strategies (which also consist of lying, swindling, cunning, deception, etc.) are commonly used by psychopaths in their everyday lives and normally work well for them, particularly in gaining access to mates and resources necessary for survival (Hare, 1993). It is the responsibility of the parents to teach their children not to allow anyone to touch them in any inappropriate way. Teach your children of the potential danger of abuse and how to avoid it. Be aware of warning signs, such as an abrupt change in a child's behavior, which may signal a problem and be alert to a child's unsettled feelings and identify their origin (Scott, 2008).

This writer's personal journey in booking and analyzing psychopathy has led to a cathartic and eye-opening revelation. Had this disorder been recognized or diagnosed before this writer's unfortunate experiences as an innocent child, it would have saved this writer from mental anguish and psychological fallout. Conflict resolution for this situation can only happen when family members such as a mother, brothers and close relatives understand and recognize the pathology of personality disorder such as psychopathy. To prevent and avoid a recurrence of the incidences which occurred to this writer, an intervention of sorts must be conducted to expose the middle male disorder.

Should this conflict resolution occur, the ability to the see "the other side of reality" is what will save us from the attacks of a psychopath? We need to see them for what they are and not for what they try to represent. The present is important; the past is gone; working on the traumas of the past makes us a better person for society today. Once we come to the realization of what has happened to us, we cannot harm ourselves anymore. It is time to recover and become the new you.

Hervey Cleckley's List of Psychopathy Symptoms:

http://psychopathyawareness.wordpress.com/category/intimidation/

1. Considerable superficial charm and average or above average intelligence.

2. Absence of delusions and other signs of irrational thinking.

3. Absence of anxiety or other "neurotic" symptoms. Considerable poise, calmness and verbal facility.

4. Unreliability, disregard for obligations, no sense of responsibility, in matters of little and great import.

5. Untruthfulness and insincerity.

6. Antisocial behavior which is inadequately motivated and poorly planned, seeming to stem from an inexplicable impulsiveness.

7. Inadequately motivated antisocial behavior.

8. Poor judgment and failure to learn from experience.

9. Pathological egocentricity. Total self-centeredness and an incapacity for real love and attachment.

10. General poverty of deep and lasting emotions.

11. Lack of any true insight; inability to see oneself as others do.

12. Ingratitude for any special considerations, kindness and trust.

13. Fantastic and objectionable behavior, after drinking and sometimes even when not drinking. Vulgarity, rudeness, quick mood shifts, pranks for facile entertainment.

14. No history of genuine suicide attempts.

15. An impersonal, trivial, and poorly integrated sex life.

16. Failure to have a life plan and to live in any ordered way (unless it is for destructive purposes or a sham).

Robert Hare's Checklist of Psychopathy Symptoms:

1. GLIB AND SUPERFICIAL CHARM — the tendency to be smooth, engaging, charming, slick, and verbally facile. Psychopathic charm is not in the least shy, self-conscious, or afraid to say anything. A psychopath never gets tongue-tied. He can also be a great listener, to simulate empathy while zeroing in on his targets' dreams and vulnerabilities, to be able to manipulate them better.

2. GRANDIOSE SELF-WORTH — a grossly inflated view of one's abilities and self-worth, self-assured, opinionated, cocky, a braggart.

Psychopaths are arrogant people who believe they are superior human beings.

3. NEED FOR STIMULATION or PRONENESS TO BOREDOM — an excessive need for novel, thrilling, and exciting stimulation; taking chances and doing things that are risky. Psychopaths often have a low self-discipline in carrying tasks through to completion because they get bored easily. They fail to work at the same job for any length of time, for example, or to finish tasks that they consider dull or routine.

4. PATHOLOGICAL LYING — can be moderate or high; in moderate form, they will be shrewd, crafty, cunning, sly, and clever; in extreme form, they will be deceptive, deceitful, underhanded, unscrupulous, manipulative and dishonest.

5. CONNING AND MANIPULATIVENESS: the use of deceit and deception to cheat, con, or defraud others for personal gain; distinguished from Item #4 in the degree to which exploitation and callous ruthlessness is present, as reflected in a lack of concern for the feelings and suffering of one's victims.

6. *LACK OF REMORSE OR GUILT: a lack of feelings or concern for the losses, pain, and suffering of victims; a tendency to be unconcerned, dispassionate, coldhearted and lack of empathy. This item is usually demonstrated by a disdain for one's victims.*

7. *SHALLOW AFFECT: emotional poverty or a limited range or depth of feelings; interpersonal coldness despite signs of open gregariousness and superficial warmth.*

8. *CALLOUSNESS and LACK OF EMPATHY: a lack of feelings toward people in general; cold, contemptuous, inconsiderate, and tactless.*

9. *PARASITIC LIFESTYLE: an intentional, manipulative, selfish, and exploitative financial dependence on others as reflected in a lack of motivation, low self-discipline and the inability to carry through one's responsibilities.*

10. *POOR BEHAVIORAL CONTROLS: expressions of irritability, annoyance, impatience, threats, aggression and verbal abuse; inadequate control of anger and temper; acting hastily.*

11. PROMISCUOUS SEXUAL BEHAVIOR: a variety of brief, superficial relations, numerous affairs, and an indiscriminate selection of sexual partners; the maintenance of numerous, multiple relationships at the same time; a history of attempts to sexually coerce others into sexual activity (rape) or taking great pride at discussing sexual exploits and conquests.

12. EARLY BEHAVIOR PROBLEMS: a variety of behaviors prior to age 13, including lying, theft, cheating, vandalism, bullying, sexual activity, fire-setting, glue-sniffing, alcohol use and running away from home.

13. LACK OF REALISTIC, LONG-TERM GOALS: an inability or persistent failure to develop and execute long-term plans and goals; a nomadic existence, aimless, lacking direction in life.

14. IMPULSIVITY: the occurrence of behaviors that are unpremeditated and lack reflection or planning; inability to resist temptation, frustrations and momentary urges; a lack of deliberation without considering the consequences; foolhardy, rash, unpredictable, erratic and reckless.

15. IRRESPONSIBILITY: repeated failure to fulfill or honor obligations and commitments; such as not paying bills, defaulting on loans, performing sloppy work, being absent or late to work, failing to honor contractual agreements.

16. FAILURE TO ACCEPT RESPONSIBILITY FOR OWN ACTIONS: a failure to accept responsibility for one's actions reflected in low conscientiousness, an absence of dutifulness, antagonistic manipulation, denial of responsibility, and an effort to manipulate others through this denial.

17. MANY SHORT-TERM RELATIONSHIPS: a lack of commitment to a long-term relationship reflected in inconsistent, undependable, and unreliable commitments in life, including in marital and familial bonds.

18. JUVENILE DELINQUENCY: behavior problems between the ages of 13-18; mostly behaviors that are crimes or clearly involve aspects of antagonism, exploitation, aggression, manipulation, or a callous, ruthless tough-mindedness.

19. REVOCATION OF CONDITION RELEASE: a revocation of probation or other conditional release due to technical violations, such as carelessness, low deliberation or failing to appear.

20. CRIMINAL VERSATILITY: a diversity of types of criminal offenses, regardless if the person has been arrested or convicted for them; taking great pride at getting away with crimes or wrongdoings.

References:

Cleckley, H. (1988). *The Mask of Sanity*. Augusta, Georgia: Hervey Milton.

Grondahl, P. (2006, August 13). *Porco labeled a psycho killer.* . Retrieved July 10, 2012, from Times Union: http://www.timesunion.com/AspStories/story.asp?storyID=508011&catego ry=PORCO&BCCode=&newsdate=9/9/2009.

Hare, R. (1999). *Without Conscience: The disturbing world of the psychopaths amoung us.* New York: Guilford Press.

Hare, R. (2003). *Technical Manual For The Revised Psychopathy Checklist 2nd ed.* . New York: Multi Health Systems.

Karpman, B. (1941). On the need of separating psychopathy into two distinct clinical subtypes:The symptomatic and the idiopathic. *Journal of Criminal Psychopathology, 3,* 112-137.

Lykken, D. T. (1995). *The Antisocial Personalities.* Hillsdale, NJ: Lawrence Erlbaum Associates.

Neumann, C. (2007). The super ordinate nature of the psychopathy checklist revised. *Journal of Personality Disorders, 21(2),* 102-117.

Pearson, P. (1998). *When she was bad: how and why women get away with murder.* Vintage, Canada: Canadian Cataloguing in Publication Data.

Samenow, S. (1984). *Inside the Criminal Mind.* Times Books.

Scott, R. G. (2008, April 5). *To Heal the Tragic Consequences of Abuse.* Retrieved July 14, 2012, from The Church of Jesus Christ of Latter Day Saints: http://www.lds.org/general-conference/2008/04/to-heal-the-shattering-consequences-of-abuse?lang=eng.

Shohov, S. (2002). *Advances in Psychology Book, Volume 15.* Hauppauge, New York: Nova Science Publisher, Inc.

Van Dam, C. (2006). *The Socially Skilled Child Molesters.* New York: The Haworth Press, Inc.